THE PATH TO HAPPINESS

Abd Ar-Rahman bin
Abd Al-Kareem Ash-Sheha

In the name of Allah, the Beneficent, the Merciful.

Dear Reader,

Islam is a complete and integral Divine religion and way of life. It has a complete code of ethics for a happy life, as well as a peaceful and tranquil life after death. Islam is free from all imperfections and defects.
Any deviant or abnormal behavior observed in a Muslim should have no bearing on Islam, none whatsoever.
The reason for such deviant behavior is generally a poor understanding of the faith, and in other cases, weak faith that leads to the person going astray from what is proper and noble.
It is unjust and unreasonable for Islam to be assessed or evaluated based on any individuals' behavior or attitudes, with the exception of the Prophet Muhammad, who is the best example and role model for all humans.

TABLE OF CONTENTS

1. Introduction	07
2. True Happiness	11
3. Benefits of the Islamic Way of Life.	21
4. How to attain True Happiness	27
6. Final Thoughts	69

FOREWORD

Osoul Center

This book has been conceived, prepared and designed by the Osoul Centre. All photos used in the book belong to the Osoul Centre. The Centre hereby permits all Sunni Muslims to reprint and publish the book in any method and format on condition that 1) acknowledgement of the Osoul Centre is clearly stated on all editions; and 2) no alteration or amendment of the text is introduced without reference to the Osoul Centre. In the case of reprinting this book, the Centre strongly recommends maintaining high quality.

- +966 504 442 532
- +966 11 445 4900
- +966 11 497 0126
- P.O.Box 29465, Riyadh 11457
- osoul@rabwah.com
- www.osoulcenter.com

All praise be to God, the Lord of all the worlds, the Creator of the heavens and earth and all creatures living in them. May God grant peace and blessings to Prophet Muhammad, God's final Messenger, whose message brought mercy to all mankind. May He also give His blessings to all the prophets and messengers whom He sent to guide mankind out of darkness and into light.

At the Osoul Centre for Islamic Advocacy, every new release that we produce gives us a great opportunity to interact with our readers. All our releases have the same overall objective; to present Islam to mankind, as it truly is. We aim to make people aware of Islam's fine aspects and profound teachings and to show clearly that it is the only faith that provides practical and effective solutions to all the problems faced by humanity. Islam gives clear and solid answers to all of the questions that have troubled people over many generations, such as: How did we come into existence and why do we exist? Where do we go from here? Furthermore, Islam is the only religion that requires its followers to love and respect all the prophets God sent, particularly Moses and Jesus (peace be upon them both).

We take great care to provide solid and rational proofs for our arguments, so as to give our readers the reassurance they need, and our releases also refute the accusations levelled against Islam and provide clarification to people's misunderstandings of Islamic teachings.

By God's grace, Islam is the fastest growing religion in our time, as confirmed by a study undertaken by the Pew Research Center,[1] and our motive is to make this great divine faith known to all people.

This book, *The Path to Happiness*, explains that the way of life provided by Islam for its followers is divine, intended to ensure that people enjoy real happiness in this present life and in the life to come. Whatever the Islamic way of life includes of obligations and prohibitions meets human needs and ensures man's happiness. Islam gives its followers a clear concept of man's status and his relationship with the universe around him. Islamic obligations and prohibitions neither restrict people's freedom, nor impose a burden on them.

Islam establishes the concept of true and everlasting happiness, which is the happy future life in heaven. This makes Muslims aspire to the sublime through the obedience of God and earning His pleasure.

We hope that readers will find this book useful in adding to their knowledge and understanding of Islam.

Basil ibn Abdullah al-Fawzan
Executive Director

---

(1) "The Future of the Global Muslim Population", Pew Research Center, 27 January 2011, Available at http://www.pewresearch.org/

Glossary

1. Dinar & Dirham: Silver and gold coins used in the past.
2. Hadeeth: Recorded reports regarding what the Prophet said, did, approved, and disapproved of, explicitly or implicitly.
3. I'tikaaf: In general, it refers to seclusion. I'tikaaf is an act of worship whereby the person secludes himself in the Masjid and worships Allah.
4. Iman: Belief.
5. Jannah: This is the Heavenly Abode or Heavenly Gardens which Allah grants His pious servants in the Hereafter.
6. Shaitan: Satan.
7. Shari'ah: Islamic Jurisprudential Law.
8. Sunnah: Has more than one meaning. It may refer to:
   a. Prophetic Traditions.
   b. A class of ruling which denotes that an act is recommended but not obligatory.

Introduction  01

Introduction

All praise is due to Allah alone, and may Allah exalt the mention of our Prophet and render him, his household and his companions safe from every evil.

You may very well find the key to your happiness by spending a few minutes reading through this booklet, so put aside any preconceived notions till you completely read through it.

Dear reader, I think you will agree with me that we live in a beautiful world that is worthy of contemplation. The creatures that dwell within it, the intricate correlation of planets, heavenly bodies and galaxies that can be witnessed are proof enough that if there were no Creator everything would fall into chaos! God, the Exalted, says:

"It is not possible for the sun to reach the moon, nor does the night overtake the day, but each, in an orbit, is swimming." (36:40)

These heavenly bodies will continue in their orbits until the Creator ordains that they are to stop, at which point chaos would spread; marking the end of this life as we know it. God, the Exalted, says:

"When the sky breaks apart and when the stars fall, scattering and when the seas erupt and when the [contents of] graves are scattered." (82:1-4)

Before we continue, a question must be asked...What is the purpose behind the creation of all of this? Was it created without purpose? How about the amazing human being regarding which God, the Exalted, says:

"O mankind, what has deceived you concerning your Lord, the Generous, Who created you, proportioned you, and balanced you? In whatever form He willed has He assembled you." (82:6-8)

Throughout the course of our lives, much of what we do is done with purpose and intention so that we can achieve our goals. Similarly, nothing God does is without a divine wisdom and purpose. He, the Exalted, says:

"Then did you think that We created you uselessly and that to Us you would not be returned? So exalted is Allah, the Sovereign, the Truth; there is no deity except Him, Lord of the Noble Throne." (23:115-116)

The world around us and the heavens above us are ample

---

(1) The actual word used in the Qur'an is Rubb. There is no proper equivalent for Rubb in the English language. It means the Creator, the Fashioner, the Provider, the One upon Whom all creatures depend for their means of subsistence, and the One Who gives life and causes death.

enough to compel us to ask the logical question, who created and perfected all of this? The untainted human nature and sane intellect will lead one to recognize his Lord as the Supreme Creator. God, the Exalted, says:

The world around us and the heavens above us are ample enough to compel us to ask the logical question, who created and perfected all of this?

"Those who remember Allah while standing or sitting or lying on their sides and give thought to the creation of the heavens and the earth, [saying], 'Our Lord, You did not create this aimlessly, exalted are You [above such a thing]. Hence, protect us from the punishment of the fire.'" (3:191)

The One Who created this universe from nothing will bring it to an end so that the eternal life may begin. Allah, the Exalted, says: "The Day when We will fold the heaven like the folding of a scroll for the [keeping of] records. As We began the first creation, we will repeat it. That is a promise binding upon Us. Indeed, we will do it." (21:104)

You, a human being, are subject to the rules of this universe, where everything has an end. You will depart this life, but in your case, the story doesn't end there as you shall be resurrected and held accountable for your deeds. After the judgment, you will go forth to everlasting bliss or end up in an abyss of endless torment. Indeed, the One Who created you from nothing can easily recreate you. Allah, the Exalted, says:

"And it is He who begins creation, then He repeats it, and that is even easier for Him. To Him belongs the paramount attribute in the heavens and earth. And He is the Exalted in Might, the Wise." (30:27)

Some may think this an improbability, but look around you. Look at the desert wastelands that do not receive a single drop of water, not a single sign of life can be seen, but behold! When rain falls and the earth is quenched, vegetation shoots forth, dismissing any wrong notions one might have had that vegetation could not be sustained in that area. This is a sure sign that resurrection is inevitable. Allah, the Exalted, says: "And of His signs is that you see the earth stilled, but when We send down upon it rain, it quivers and grows. Indeed, He who has given it life is the Giver of Life to the dead. Indeed, He is over all things competent." (41:39)

True Happiness 02

Psychologists define happiness as a continuous feeling of enjoyment, satisfaction, generosity and delight, arising from contentment in one's self and life, as well as the belief that they will have a blissful destiny

True Happiness

Do you know what is happiness? It has been defined as an agreeable feeling or condition of the soul arising from good fortune of any kind that is built on firm belief.

Every person must have a goal they wish to attain. The more success they have toward accomplishing this goal, the greater their sense of happiness.

Psychologists define happiness as a continuous feeling of enjoyment, satisfaction, generosity and delight, arising from contentment in one's self and life, as well as the belief that they will have a blissful destiny.

Types of Happiness

From this definition, we can categorize happiness into three categories:

First Category: False happiness, which lasts only for a short period of time. This form of happiness is the result of a sudden, but often short-lived, "high". Many believe that happiness can be attained through substance abuse and, on account of this, they consume drugs and alcohol to avoid the problems of everyday life. They believe happiness is achieved initially by forgetting about the problems of life. Drug abuse gives one an illusion of happiness, which quickly dissipates along with the amount of drug in the bloodstream, plunging that individual into a state of complete misery. This would then drive that person to seek out more drugs, and ultimately become addicted and vulnerable. Furthermore, this individual is at risk for contracting a number of psychological and physical diseases.

Second Category: Happiness experienced when achieving goals. It is similar to the previous form of happiness in that it is short-lived, although it is less harmful than the previous form of happiness. Great efforts are exerted in attaining a goal, and when it is finally achieved, one would wonder, what's next? The emptiness one would experience after the climax and initial bout of happiness is somewhat similar to the emptiness experienced in the first category.

True happiness. This form of happiness will remain with an individual under all circumstances; through delight and anguish, poverty and prosperity, sickness and health.

Third Category: True happiness. This form of happiness will remain with an individual under all circumstances; through delight and anguish, poverty and prosperity, sickness and health and whether or not one would attain of this world what they wish for or not. This happiness is the result of one's belief.

Do you want true Happiness?

This question may seem odd, since the answer is obvious.

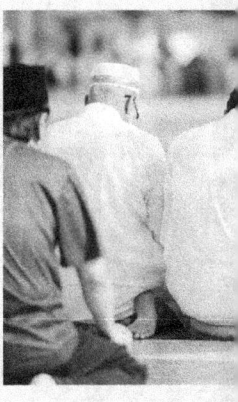

I believe any sane individual would reply in the affirmative. So how can one achieve happiness? Every individual has their own opinion as regards how they can attain happiness. Some believe that happiness is attained by making money, while others see it in holding positions of power. It is sometimes seen through having many friends or having the power to influence others. If we were to ask anyone who has strived to achieve a goal, if they have actually attained true happiness, the answer would most often be in the negative. The reason is simple; true happiness is a continuous feeling of bliss and comfort. One will not be able to experience this even if they had an earth-load of gold, for as it has been said in an Arabic proverb, "One may be able to purchase a bed, but certainly cannot purchase sleep."

Many times, one's faith will distance one from true happiness because it may require of a person to believe in the illogical or unreasonable. The spiritual vacuum that leads one to misery

Attaining true happiness is easy, within anyone's reach, but the source from which it can be acquired may remain a puzzle to many.

cannot be removed unless one accepts the true faith, which will contribute to his individuality and define for him a worthy goal in life.

Attaining true happiness is actually easy and well within anyone's reach, but the source from which it can be acquired remains a puzzle to many. If one is truly searching for happiness, they should be willing to sacrifice in order to attain it. True happiness can only be acquired by accepting Islam; by submitting yourself to the Creator. Some may view this statement with skepticism, but it is the truth. Once a person accepts Islam wholeheartedly and begins to apply it as they should and upholds its commandments as per its two sources, the Qur'an and Sunnah[1], they will experience true happiness.

Some people may ask, "Why?" Before answering, an examination of the definition of happiness is required. Psychologists state that happiness is a continuous feeling of enjoyment, satisfaction, generosity and delight arising from contentment in one's self, life and ultimate destiny. An individual will achieve all of this through Islam. God, Almighty, says:

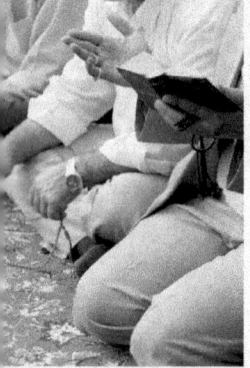

"Indeed, the Muslim men and Muslim women, the believing men and believing women, the obedient men and obedient women, the truthful men and the truthful women, the patient men and the patient women, the humble men and the humble women, the fasting men and the fasting women, the men who guard their private parts and the women who do so, and the men who remember Allah often and the women who do so - for them Allah has prepared forgiveness and a great reward." (33:35)

Satisfaction in life is also guaranteed by Almighty God:

"You are the best nation produced for mankind. You enjoin what is right, forbid what is wrong, and believe in Allah. If only the People of the Scripture had believed, it would have been better for them. Among them are believers, but most of them are defiantly disobedient." (3:110)

(1) The Sunnah is the Prophetic Traditions. They include the Prophet's actions, statements and tacit approvals.

Satisfaction is also promised to us by Almighty God in the next life, He says:
"Indeed, those who have believed and done righteous deeds - they will have the Gardens of Paradise[1] as their home. Therein they shall abide forever. They will never desire to leave it." (18:107-108)

- You are the best nation produced (3:110)

In essence, true happiness is the result of a number of factors and cannot be achieved except when one accepts a faith that balances between the material and spiritual aspects of life. Worldly "man-made" systems, new-age faiths and cults that are marketed to the masses; all are adopted as a reaction to Islam. Yet, these systems offer no long-term solutions to the problems we face today. Consider for a moment the collapsed Soviet Union, and the currently reigning capitalist systems that are on the brink of collapse. The reason that these systems have not succeeded is simple; they are built upon false doctrines and are based on opinions that are short-sighted.

For the most part, "man-made" systems typically favor one group of people over others. They promote one of two extremes, the individual over the community or community over the individual. What is worse than this, is that many "man-made" systems will favor the material aspect of life over the spiritual one. Islam, on the other hand, presents mankind with a perfect equilibrium. God, the Exalted, says:
"And thus we have made you a moderate community such that you will be witnesses over the people and the Messenger will be a witness over you." (2:143)

Prophet Muhammad [2] told his companion Abdullah b. Umar, may Allah be pleased with him:

(1) This is the Heavenly Abode or Heavenly Gardens, which Allah grants His pious servants in the Hereafter.

(2) This symbol means, "may Allah exalt his mention, and render him and his household safe and secure from every derogatory thing".

Materialists tend to disregard the soul and view life as nothing but a means through which they can satisfy their desires. They absolutely disregard the spiritual side of life.

"O Abdullah I have been informed that you continuously fast throughout the days and perform prayers throughout the night.' He said: 'Yes, I do that.' The Prophet (ﷺ) said to him: 'Do not do that, fast a day and do not fast the next, perform prayers for a period of time during the night and then get some sleep. For indeed, your body has a right over you, your eyes have a right over you and your wife has a right over you." (Bukhari)

Materialists tend to disregard the soul and view life as nothing but a means through which they can satisfy their various appetites. They absolutely disregard the spiritual side of life. This is the common trend in the West, for many have abandoned religion. The question that should be asked then is, will this bring about happiness? Any logical, sane individual will find the answer to this to be in the negative. If material comforts were the key to happiness, affluent individuals wouldn't commit suicide as happens in many of the richest and most developed societies in the world today. Whereas, the opposite is not true - those living in the poorest societies in the world often display a deep happiness and contentment with their life.

Sadness thus comes directly as a result of the emptiness of the soul; a spiritual disease. The cure, quite simple and free of charge, is to believe in God Almighty and to accept the faith that He has approved for mankind. This spiritual disease, if left unattended, will have disastrous consequences, as can be seen in many shattered lives around the world.

In Scandinavia, a first world nation, which is considered by some to be amongst the wealthiest of countries in the world, both on the individual basis and governmental level, one would think people would be living blissful lives. Strangely enough, it has the highest suicide rate in the world. Muslim countries, many of which are considered of the "third-world" block, have such a small percentage of suicides that they number less than one case per month in many cases.

F. Filweas[(1)] said: "The West is suffering from a vast spiritual void, which no principle or faith could fill to bring about happiness. Despite the affluence there, and the so-called economic prosperity, besides the satisfaction of physical needs of people, the Western man still has a sense of worthlessness in his life. He wonders why he is living, where he is going, and why. But no one so far has given him a satisfactory response. Unfortunately, he has no idea that his remedy is in the right religion about which he knows nothing more than doubts. However, the beginning of a light has started to breakthrough after a few groups of Westerners embraced Islam and Western man began to see men and women put Islam into practice and live up to its teachings with his own eyes. Everyday some people there embrace the true religion. It is just the beginning."

The West is suffering from a vast spiritual void, which no principle or faith could fill to bring about happiness.

The soul should be fed as should the body. If this is not done properly, one will have unnecessary anxiety, feelings of discontent and general unhappiness. The soul is nourished with the true belief in the Oneness of God, and the belief that He will resurrect us and hold us accountable for what we have done. One must also excel in doing the good and avoiding the evil. God, Almighty, says:
"Those who have believed and whose hearts are assured by the remembrance of Allah. Unquestionably, by the remembrance of Allah hearts are assured." (13:28)

Contentment, happiness, and feelings of bliss, are some of the great feelings a sincere Muslim experiences on a regular basis. The scholar, Ibn Taymiyyah, may God have mercy on him, after being tortured, banished and imprisoned said: "What can my enemies do to me? My paradise and orchard are in my heart and they never part with me. If my captors imprison me, I see it as a religious retreat, if they kill me it is martyrdom, and if they banish me from my land it is like tourism."

(1) A British Naval officer who participated in both world wars and embraced Islam in 1924 after he had read the Holy Qur'an and some books on Islam.

The teachings of Islam will most certainly cause you to forget your worries and will make you patient. It will move you from the sphere of discontentment to one of contentment.

These words are simply amazing. He was imprisoned and mistreated and still, this is what he felt. A person true in his faith will be happy at all times. Islam will give a person complete spiritual happiness and contentment regardless of their financial or social condition in life. A true Muslim will be content in almost all circumstances, whether sick or healthy, rich or poor, or in a state of security or chaos. God, the Exalted, says:

"When disaster strikes them, they say, 'Indeed we belong to Allah, and indeed to Him we will return.' Those are the ones upon whom are blessings from their Lord and mercy, and it is those who are the rightly guided." (2:156-157)

The Messenger of God ﷺ said:

"Amazing indeed is the attitude of the believer, everything is ultimately good for him and this is only for a believer. When he is graced with a blessing, he would be thankful and grateful to God and it would be good for him, and when he is afflicted with a calamity, he would be patient and it would be good for him." (Muslim)

The teachings of Islam will most certainly cause you to forget your worries and will make you patient. It will move you from the sphere of discontentment to one of contentment.

It is also important to remember that Islam does not order its followers to become monks or to distance themselves from worldly pleasures. On the contrary, it requires of a believer to utilize whatever worldly possessions they have to acquire true happiness.

Whoever has a position of power should use his power to spread the justice found in the religion of God and to take care of the needs of his fellow brothers and sisters. God says:

"Whoever intercedes for a good cause will have a reward therefrom, and whoever intercedes for an evil cause will have a burden therefrom. And ever is Allah, over all things, a Keeper." (4:85)

Whoever has wealth should use that wealth in the path of God and to help alleviate the problems of his fellow brothers. God says:

"And those who know that as regards their wealth, both the petitioner and the deprived have rights." (70:24-5)

The Prophet ﷺ clarified what will happen with one's wealth. He said:

"The [person] will say, 'My wealth, my wealth.' It will be said, 'Your wealth is none other than that which you consumed and it turned to waste, or that which you wore and wore it out, or that which you gave in charity and stored it away for yourself [in the Hereafter].'" (Muslim)

The Messenger of Allah ﷺ is the example for all Muslims and every Muslim tries hard to emulate him. Abu Dharr, one of the Companions of the Prophet, said, "I was walking with the Prophet ﷺ in Madinah till we reached Mount Uhud." The Prophet ﷺ said:

"O Abu Dharr!' I replied, 'Yes O Messenger of Allah.' He said, 'If I had a mountain of gold the size of Mount Uhud, I would distribute it all within three days, and would only take from it enough to pay off a debt.' The Prophet (ﷺ) then said, 'Those who are the richest in this world will be the poorest on the Day of Resurrection, except if they give out in charity and indeed very few are they.'" (Bukhari)

> **The Messenger** of Allah ﷺ is the example for all Muslims and every Muslim tries hard to emulate him.

> • "Those who have believed and whose hearts are assured by the remembrance of Allah." (13:28)

Benefits of the Islamic Way of Life

03

The Path To Happiness

Any aware individual will know that interest is a form of injustice through which the wealthy consume the wealth of the less fortunate.

The Islamic way of life is indeed one that will achieve for its follower's true happiness, on the condition that one follows its commandments and refrains from its prohibitions. One is not deprived by the commandments of Islam. On the contrary, it is a divine system of law given to us by the Creator of man. He knows best what will benefit us in this world. Let us view some of these commandments and see whether or not they are beneficial.

01. Usury:

God, Almighty, says:

"O you who have believed, fear Allah and give up what remains [due to you] of interest, if you are sincerely believers." (2:278)

Almost everyone knows that interest is a form of injustice through which the rich consume the wealth of the poor. In short, it is a disgusting form of greed that exploits the weaknesses of people. From an economical perspective, it places wealth in the hands of a few. Many non-Muslims have spoken out against this system and have confirmed its flaws.

02. Fornication and Adultery:

Whoever lives in Western society will know full well the grave dangers that pertain to sexual freedom. The dangers include a number of sexually transmitted diseases that have sadly become quite widespread. God, the Exalted, says:

"And do not approach fornication and adultery. Indeed, it is ever an immorality and is evil as a way." (17:32)

The Prophet ﷺ said:

"If fornication and adultery become widespread among a people, diseases will spread amongst them that were not known in previous generations." (Ibn Majah)

Benefits of the Islamic Way of Life

◆ **Drinking Alcohol:** The dangers of alcohol have been affirmed by modern medicine. God, Almighty, says: "O you who have believed, indeed, intoxicants, gambling, [sacrificing on] stone alters, and divining arrows are but defilement from the work of Satan, so avoid it that you may be successful. Satan only wants to cause between you animosity and hatred through intoxicants and gambling and to avert you from the remembrance of Allah and from prayer. So will you not desist?" (5:90-91)

There are a number of medical reasons for the prohibition of the consumption of alcohol. Millions of people die every year as a result of it.

There are a number of medical reasons for the prohibition of the consumption of alcohol. Millions of people die every year as a result of it. Some alcohol related illnesses include:

- Liver failure.
- Various forms of cancer.
- Esophagitis, gastritis, pancreatitis and hepatitis.
- Cardiomyopathy.
- Seizures.
- Brain damage and dementia.
- Anemia, jaundice and blood abnormalities.
- Fetal Alcohol Syndrome.

◆ **Castigatory laws:** God, Almighty, says:
"And there is for you, in legal retribution, [the saving of] life, O people of understanding, that you may become righteous." (2:179)

God, Almighty, has most certainly told the truth. When castigatory punishments are implemented, it would save people's lives and protect society at large. It would also protect people's wealth and honor.

In order for any system to be successful, there must be an influential power to support it. People would freely go through red lights if no system were in place to punish those who do so. People would steal if no deterrent was present. In short, there must be a significant deterrent in place. If no such deterrent is present, chaos will become widespread.

Applying castigatory law is nothing new. It was common amongst previous divine systems of law. God, the All-Wise, says:
"And We ordained for them therein a life for a life, an eye for an eye, a nose for a nose, an ear for an ear, a tooth for a tooth, and for wounds, legal retribution. But whoever gives [up his right as] charity, it is an expiation for him. And whoever does not judge by what Allah has revealed - then it is those who are the wrongdoers." (5:45)

Man-made laws give more priority to the oppressor than to the oppressed. They can often be worked around and one can be saved from the punishment. No system of law in this age has proven to be as effective as Islam.

The question arises of which form of castigatory punishment is more effective in alleviating crime in society. Are the divine castigatory laws handed down by the Creator above those found within man-made systems of law? Man-made laws give more priority to the oppressor than to the oppressed. They can often be worked around, and one can be saved from the punishment. No system of law in this age has proven to be as effective as Islam.

• And there is for you in legal retribution [saving of] life (2:17)

How to Attain True Happiness?

04

The Path To Happiness

With the belief in God, one will attain true happiness. When one is faced with trials, he asks God directly to alleviate the problems that he faces.

True happiness is attained through a number of key fundamental beliefs:

The First Pillar: Belief in God and in His Oneness

Whoever believes in Allah and in His Oneness will be guided to the path of happiness. His heart will be content, and he will live in a state of pure tranquility. God, Almighty, says:

"Those who have believed and whose hearts are assured by the remembrance of Allah. Unquestionably, by the remembrance of Allah hearts are assured." (13:28)

When man knows the greatness of His creator who has created all things and is capable over all things, he will become more humble. Nothing is like unto Him. God, Almighty, says:

"Allah - there is no deity except Him, the Ever-Living, the Sustainer of [all] existence. Neither drowsiness overtakes Him nor sleep. To Him belongs whatever is in the heavens and whatever is on the earth. Who is it that can intercede with Him except by His permission? He knows what is [presently] before them and what will be after them, and they encompass not a thing of His knowledge except for what He wills. His footstool extends over the heavens and the earth, and their preservation tires Him not. And He is the Most High, the Most Great." (2:255)

With the belief in God, one will attain true happiness. When one is faced with trials, he asks God directly to alleviate the problems that he faces. God says:

I am near. I respond to the invocation of the supplicant when he calls upon Me (2:186)

"And when My slaves ask you, [O Muhammad], concerning Me - indeed I am near. I respond to the supplicant when he calls upon Me. So let them respond to me and believe in Me that they may be guided." (2:186)

Misery is the result of one not believing in God, the Almighty. Whoever does not believe in God will indeed live a life filled with anxiety and misery. God instilled in us a natural disposition to recognize the Creator of the Heavens and the Earth. God can easily be recognized by simple deductions, as is mentioned in the following verse:

"Or were they created by nothing, or were they the creators [of themselves]?" (52:35)

One's belief in God must be tied with the belief in the Oneness of God. One must not associate any partners with Him. Whoever associates a partner with God, his belief will not benefit him.

One's belief in God must be tied with the belief in the Oneness of God. One must not associate any partners with Him. Whoever associates a partner with God, his belief will not benefit him. God, Almighty, says:

"Indeed, Allah does not forgive associating others in worship with Him, but He forgives what is less than that for whom He wills. And he who associates in worship others with Allah has certainly fabricated a tremendous sin." (4:48)

When one associates in worship others with God, they would be disrespecting God. Anything imperfect deserves no form of divine praise, let alone worship! God, Almighty, says:

"Had there been within the Heavens and Earth gods besides Allah, they would both have been ruined. So exalted is Allah, Lord of the Throne, above what they describe." (21:22)

God, the Exalted, is not in need of any of His creation; whereas, all creation is in need of Him. God, Almighty, says:

"Allah has not taken any son, nor has there ever been with Him any deity. If there had been, then each deity would have taken what it created, and some of them would have sought to overcome others. Exalted is Allah above what they attribute to Him." (23:91)

> **When** one fears others than God, it will bring him misery. Satan will strike fear in his heart.

Of the Benefits of the Belief in God:

01 It will free one from all forms of enslavement to any creature. When one is fully cognizant that fate is in the hands of God and can only be changed by His will, they will ultimately free themselves from all forms of spiritual slavery and will worship and submit to their Creator fully. God, the Exalted, says:
"Say, 'Who is Lord of the heavens and earth?' Say, 'Allah.' Say, 'Have you then taken besides Him allies not possessing [even] for themselves any benefit or any harm?' Say, 'Is the blind equivalent to the seeing? Or is darkness equivalent to light? Or have they attributed to Allah partners who created like His creation so that the creation [of each] seemed similar to them?' Say, 'Allah is the Creator of all things, and He is the One, the Prevailing.'" (13:16)

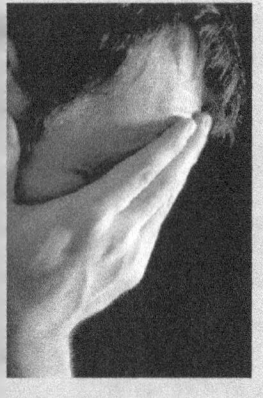

02 Each individual will fear God alone. When one fears others than God, it will bring him misery. Satan will strike fear in his heart. Allah says:
"That is only Satan who frightens [you] of his supporters. So fear them not, but fear Me, if you are [indeed] believers." (3:175)

03 One will become courageous and brave. Allah causes death and appoints for each person a period for which they will live on this earth. God, Almighty, says:
"And it is not [possible] for one to die except by the permission of Allah at a decree determined." (3:145)

As for a non-believer, they will live a life of misery because disbelief does not give a person anything to fall back on in times of hardship. How true are the words of God, the Almighty, when He says:
"So whoever Allah wants to guide - He expands his chest to [contain] Islam. And whoever He wants to misguide - He makes his chest tight and constricted as though he were climbing into the sky. Thus does Allah place defilement upon those who do not believe." (6:125)

- So whoever Allah wants to guide - He expands his chest to Islam (6:125)

The Second Pillar: Belief in the Angels

Angels are of the unseen world. One can only understand their nature by hearing what the Messengers brought to us of the revelation of God. Through them the Message of God was given to the Prophets and Messengers on Earth. The Angel in charge of delivering Divine Messages was the Angel Gabriel. God, the Exalted, says:

"O you who have believed, believe in Allah and His Messenger and the Book that He sent down upon His Messenger and the Scripture which He sent down before. And whoever disbelieves in Allah, His angels, His books, His messengers, and the Last Day has certainly gone far astray." (4:136)

> **Angels** are of the unseen world. One can only understand their nature by hearing what the Messengers brought to us of the revelation of God.

The Third Pillar: Belief in the Scriptures

These scriptures contain the instructions for life, which a believer should apply so as to succeed. When one puts the revelation of God into application, they will indeed experience social, individual and political stability. God says:

"Whoever does righteousness, whether male or female, while he is a believer - We will surely cause him to live a good life, and We will surely give them their reward [in the Hereafter] according to the best of what they used to do." (16:97)

A good life is one that includes all righteous walks of life. It will suffice one's soul and bestow true happiness upon an individual. God, Almighty, says:

"Indeed, those who have believed [in the Prophet Muhammad ﷺ] and those [before him ﷺ] who were Jews or Sabeans or Christians - those among them who believed in Allah and the Last Day and did righteousness - no fear will there be concerning them, nor will they grieve." (5:69)

The Teachings of Islam bring Happiness

The teachings of Islam have a great impact on the upbringing of a practicing Muslim. It also has an impact on his manners, ethics and, ultimately, upon his state of mind; a state of stable happiness. The teachings of Islam distance a Muslim from being miserable. These Islamic teachings include:

01 **To love Allah and His Messenger.** Loving Allah and His Messenger will motivate a believer to give charitably to attain this love. As it has been said, "True happiness has no price." The pursuit of happiness has led some to spending great amounts of money in hope of attaining the approval of a loved one. When asked if it was worth it in the end, they would certainly agree; for love has no price, and happiness is worth the price!

Loving Allah and His Messenger will provoke a believer to give out in that path to attain this love.

If this is the case with love in this life, attaining Godly love should be a goal that all strive for. God says:

"And yet, among the people are those who take other than Allah as equals [to Him]. They love them as they should love Allah. But those who believe are stronger in love for Allah. And if only those who have wronged would consider [that] when they see the punishment, [they will be certain] that all power belongs to Allah and that Allah is severe in punishment." (2:165)

The Companions of the Prophet loved Allah and His Prophet very much. When the Companion Khubaib b. Adi was brought forth to be executed by the polytheists, they asked him, "Do you have any last requests?" He said, "Yes, let me perform prayer." They allowed him to perform the prayer.

He was the first to perform a two-unit prayer before execution.

After he finished praying he said, "By Allah, if it were not for the fact that you might say, I am afraid of dying, I would have lengthened my prayer." When they wanted to execute him, they asked him, "Don't you wish that the Prophet Muhammad were in your place and that you could be safe with your family?" He replied, "By Allah, I wouldn't want Muhammad to be harmed by a thorn while I am in the safety of my family!"

The miserable is he who gives priority to his desires over the love of Allah and the Messenger. God says:
"Say, [O Muhammad], 'If your fathers, your sons, your brothers, your wives, your relatives, the wealth which you have obtained, commerce wherein you fear decline, and dwellings with which you are pleased are more beloved to you than Allah and His Messenger and striving in His cause, then wait until Allah executes His command. And Allah does not guide the defiantly disobedient people.'" (9:24)

• And Allah does not guide the defiantly disobedient people (9:24)

When one loves for the sake of Allah and His Messenger, he will gladly make many sacrifices, for this love is everlasting and a believer will feel the utmost happiness. Almighty, God says:
"And [also for] those who were settled in Madinah and [adopted] the faith before them. They love those who emigrated to them and find not any want in their hearts of what the emigrants were given, but give them preference over themselves, even though they are in need themselves. And whoever is protected from the stinginess of his soul - it is those who will be the successful." (59:9)

Achieving this love is indeed one method by which a person can protect himself from the difficulties, hardships and trials of the Day of Resurrection.

The Prophet said:

"One will experience the 'sweetness' of faith when they acquire three traits: that Allah and His Prophet are more beloved to Himself than all of creation, that one love for the sake of God, and that one hate to return to disbelief as much as they would hate to be tossed into the blazing Fire." (Bukhari)

Achieving this love is indeed one method by which a person can protect himself from the difficulties, hardships and trials of the Day of Resurrection. The Prophet said:

"Seven types of people will be shaded in the Shade of Allah, a day when there is no shade but His shade. A just ruler, a youth who grew up worshipping Allah, a man whose heart is attached to the mosque, two who loved each other for the sake of Allah and then departed on that as well, a man whom an affluent woman sought to seduce him, but he said, 'I fear Allah', a man who gave out in charity so secretly that his left hand knew not of what was in his right hand, and a man who remembered Allah and then wept." (Bukhari)

Worshipping Allah will indeed make one submissive to Allah and will free him from being a captive to his desires and whims. When a person follows that which has been ordained by Allah and abstains from the prohibited, he will feel true happiness for at that point, he will have overcome his desires and defeated Satan.

The teachings of Islam instruct us to dedicate our lives, wealth and time for the sake of God. Practicing Islam is not only a temporary effort, to be done occasionally; it is a way of life. Allah says:

"Say, 'Indeed, my prayer, my rites of sacrifice, my living and my dying are all for Allah, Lord of the worlds.'" (6:162)

How to Attain True Happiness

W. Montgomery Watt in his book, *What is Islam?*, said: "Prejudice is only one of the difficulties to be met by the European or American student of Islam. As soon as he begins to describe Islam as 'the religion of the Qur'an', or 'the religion of the four hundred million Muslims of today', he introduces a category which does not fit the category of 'religion'. For what does 'religion' now mean to the occidental? At best, for the ordinary man, it means a way of spending an hour or so on Sundays in practices which give him some support and strength in dealing with the problems of daily life, and which encourages him to be friendly towards other persons and to maintain the standards of sexual propriety; it has little or nothing to do with commerce or economics or politics or industrial relationships. At worst, it fosters an attitude of complacency in the more prosperous individuals and breeds smugness. The European may even look on religion as an opiate developed by exploiters of the common people in order to keep them in subjection. How different from the connotations to the Muslim of the verse (3:19): 'The true religion with God is Islam!' The word translated as 'religion' is Din, which, in Arabic, commonly refers to a whole way of life. It is not a private matter for individuals, touching only the periphery of their lives, but something which is both private and public, something which permeates the whole fabric of society in a way of which men are conscious. It is - all in one - theological dogma, forms of worship, political theory, and a detailed code of conduct, including even matters which the European would classify as hygiene or etiquette."[1]

W. Montgomery Watt in his book, *What is Islam?*, said: "The European may even look on religion as an opiate developed by exploiters of the common people in order to keep them in subjection."

(1) W. Montgomery Watt is a Scottish Orientalist.

The Angels, Prophets and Messengers of God were all submissive to Him. Allah says:
"Never would the Messiah disdain to be a servant of Allah, nor would the angels near [to Him]. And whoever disdains His worship and is arrogant - He will gather them to Himself all together." (4:172)

The Path To Happiness

> **Whoever** turns away from the worship of Allah will only experience a life of misery, for he will have no direction in his life and will not experience true happiness.

All creation is submissive to Allah, which proves the greatness of the Creator. Allah says:

"The seven heavens and the earth and whatever is in them exalt Him. And there is not a thing except that it exalts Allah by His praise, but you do not understand their [way of] exalting. Indeed, He is ever Forbearing and Forgiving." (17:44)

Whoever turns away from the worship of Allah will only experience a life of misery, for he will have no direction in his life and will not experience true happiness. Allah says:

"And whoever turns away from My remembrance, indeed, he will have an uneasy life, and We will raise him on the Day of Resurrection blind." (20:124)

In short, whoever is not submissive to Allah is a puppet to the Devil. Allah says:

"And whoever is blinded from remembrance of the Most Merciful, We appoint for him a devil, and he is to him a companion." (43:36)

Satan will only lead one to misery, as he himself has promised: "Iblis said, 'My Lord, because You have put me in error, I will surely make [disobedience] attractive to them on earth, and I will mislead them all.'" (15:39)

Worshipping Allah indeed bestows upon one an infinite feeling of happiness which is unparalleled. Listen to what one of the Muslims said upon expressing his feelings about the happiness that he felt:

"If the kings or their children knew of the happiness that we experience, they would indeed fight us for it with their swords."

02 What is the formula to true, ever-lasting happiness? True happiness is the result of the same actions that will also grant an individual with a blissful life in the Hereafter. This is what makes a Muslim always strive to become better. God, the Exalted says:

"And as for those who were [destined to be] prosperous, they will be in Paradise, abiding therein as long as the heavens and the earth endure, except what your Lord should will - a bestowal uninterrupted." (11:108)

One should not make an objective of amassing as much wealth as he can in this life, for the Prophet ﷺ said:
"This world is the prison of the believer and the paradise of the non-believer." (Abu Dawood)

True happiness is that which will bless an individual with a blissful life in the Hereafter. This is what makes a Muslim always strive to become better.

One may ask, "How can all of this be true when we see that many non-Muslims are living in poverty, while other Muslims are very wealthy?" The answer is simple, and can be clarified through the following story. The head judge of Egypt, Ibn Hajar al-Asqalani, may Allah have mercy on him, was stopped by a Jew who asked him, "How do you interpret the words of your Prophet ﷺ 'This world is the prison of the believer and the Paradise of the non-believer.' I am a non-believer and yet, I am very poor. You are very wealthy and are a Muslim!" Ibn Hajar replied, "Even though you are poor, you are still considered to be in your paradise, for the punishment that awaits you in the next life is extremely painful. And even though I am dressed up in these robes, if Allah wills to admit me into Jannah[1], this bliss that I am enjoying in this world is considered nothing in comparison to the joys of Jannah." Upon hearing these words, the poor man accepted Islam.

Islam instructs the believer to avoid overestimating the life of this world. Its insignificance is clarified and a Muslim is not to indulge deeply into it. In the Prophetic Tradition narrated by Sahl b. Sa'd it states: "We were with the Messenger of Allah ﷺ in the area of Dhul-Hulaifah, and he saw a bloated, dead sheep at which he said:

'Do you see the owner of this sheep bothering himself with it? By the One in Whose hands is my life, the entire world is less important to Allah than this sheep is to its owner. If this world was equal in value to the wing of a fly, Allah would not even have given a non-Muslim a drop of water.'" (Ibn Majah)

[1] Jannah is the name of the Heavenly abode in which the believers will receive eternal bliss.

03 The Messengers and the Prophets are the best of creation, and the most beloved to Allah. They were all put through trials and tribulations. Some of them were killed, banished from their homelands and rejected by their people. If this is the case, anyone less than them in rank and status may be harmed in a similar way. When a trial befalls us, we should not fret. Rather, we hold steadfast, for this is the path through which we will taste the sweetness of faith and experience true happiness.

Allah says about the Prophet Noah:

"And We certainly sent Noah to his people, and he remained among them a thousand years minus fifty years, and the flood seized them while they were wrongdoers." (29:14)

Allah says, relating to us the story of the Prophet Ibrahim:

"And the answer of Abraham's people was not but that they said, 'Kill him or burn him,' but Allah saved him from the fire. Indeed, in that are signs for a people who believe." (29:24)

Allah says about the Prophet Moses:

"And Pharaoh said, 'Let me kill Moses and let him call upon his Lord. Indeed, I fear that he will change your religion or that he will cause corruption in the land.'" (40:26)

Allah says about the Prophet Shuaib:

"We know that you, [O Muhammad], are saddened by what they say. And indeed, they do not call you untruthful, but it is the verses of Allah that the wrongdoers reject." (7:88)

Madinah SAUDI ARABIA, The Nabawi mosque is the second holiest mosque in Islam.

Allah says about the Prophet Salih:

"They said, 'O Salih, you were among us a man of promise before this. Do you forbid us to worship what our fathers worshipped? And indeed we are, about that to which you invite us, in disquieting doubt.'" (11:62)

Allah says about the Prophet Lot:

"But the answer of his people was not except that they said, 'Expel the family of Lot from your city. Indeed, they are people who would keep themselves pure.'" (27:56)

Allah says about the Prophet Jesus:

"And for their saying, 'Indeed, we have killed the Messiah, Jesus, the son of Mary, the messenger of Allah.' And they did not kill him, nor did they crucify him, but [instead] another was made to resemble him to them. And indeed, those who differ over it are in doubt about it. They have no knowledge of it except the following of assumption. And they did not kill him, for certain." (4:157)

• And they did not kill him, nor did they crucify him, but [instead] another was made to resemble him to them. (4:157)

Allah says about Prophet Muhammad:

"Said the eminent ones who were arrogant among his people, 'We will surely evict you, O Shu'aib, and those who have believed with you from our city, or you must return to our religion.' He said, 'Even if we were unwilling?'" (6:33)

• Muhammad is the Messenger of Allah

The Path To Happiness

People who live only to acquire their whims and desires, don't actually experience happiness.

04 Defining the greatest goal in the life of a Muslim. The goal of every Muslim should be to attain the mercy of Allah and His Paradise. This goal cannot be achieved except after death. The Muslim will always be in a continuous struggle till death to attain this goal. As for non-believers, they seek to achieve worldly goals and experience short-lived happiness when achieving their goals. When a person achieves the goal that he was working so hard to attain, they will then experience anxiety as to what is next. This will lead a person to become unstable in the spiritual sense of the word. People, who are of this category, those who live only to acquire their desires, don't actually experience happiness. Allah says about them:

"Allah will admit those who have believed and performed righteous deeds to gardens beneath which rivers flow, but those who disbelieve enjoy themselves and eat as grazing livestock eat, and the Fire will be their residence." (47:12)

Even if these individuals hold degrees in various fields, yet are incapable of recognizing their Lord, their knowledge would not have been of benefit to them! Allah says:

"Or do you think that most of them hear or reason? They are not except like livestock. Rather, they are [even] more astray in their way." (25:44)

It has been said by a poet, "Don't look at those who have passed away or how they passed, but look at how those that were successful became successful." Allah says:

"And We have certainly created for Hell many of the jinn and mankind. They have hearts with which they do not understand, eyes with which they do not see, and ears with which they do not hear. They are like livestock; rather, they are more astray. It is they who are the heedless." (7:179)

This does not mean that one should cast aside this worldly life and become a burden upon others. Allah has ordered that his servants strive in this world and work hard to acquire their provisions. This is something ordained in the Shari'ah⁽¹⁾. Allah says:

"It is He who made the earth subservient to you - so walk among its slopes and eat of His provision - and to Him is the resurrection." (67:15)

One's rank will be elevated when they work and strive to acquire the basic necessities of life, to feed themselves and their families and also when they give charitably for the pleasure of God. Allah says: "Those who spend their wealth in the way of Allah and then do not follow up what they have spent with reminders [of it], or [other] injury, will have their reward with their Lord, and there will be no fear concerning them, nor will they grieve." (2:262)

What is required of a Muslim is that the glitter of this life does not ruin their intention and deeds. The Prophet ﷺ said:
"The hand that gives out in charity is better than that which takes it. Give charity to those whom you support and the best form of charity is to give while you are wealthy. Whoever abstains from taking charity, Allah will bless him." (Bukhari)

A person will be rewarded for his intention. If one who is wealthy intends to give out in the path of Allah, Allah will reward him according to that intention. The Prophet ﷺ said:
"This world is for four individuals. A servant whom Allah gave wealth and knowledge and he fears Allah and maintains family relations. He understands that Allah has a right upon him. This individual is in the best of ranks. The second, a servant whom Allah gave him knowledge, but did not bestow upon him wealth, and if he is sincere in his intention, and says: 'If I had money, I would do with it as so and so is doing.' They would be equal in reward." (Tirmidthi)

A person will be rewarded for his intention. If one who is wealthy intends to give out in the path of Allah, Allah will reward him according to that intention.

• The hand that gives out in charity is better than that which takes it.

(1) Shari'ah, Islamic law.

Allah has clarified the shortness of this life. Allah has clarified that this life is only a stage to the afterlife, which is the ultimate, everlasting life.

05 Knowing the reality of this life. Islam has clarified to the Muslim that this life is nothing more than a passing pleasure. Allah says:
"Beautified for people is the love of that which they desire - of women and sons, heaped-up sums of gold and silver, fine branded horses, and cattle and tilled land. That is the enjoyment of the worldly life, but Allah has with Him the best return." (3:14)

Allah has clarified the shortness of this life, He said:
"Know that the life of this world is but amusement and diversion and adornment and boasting to one another, and competition in increase of wealth and children - like the example of a rain whose [resulting] plant growth pleases the tillers. Then it dries and you see it turned yellow, then it becomes [scattered] debris. And in the Hereafter is severe punishment and forgiveness from Allah and approval. And what is the worldly life except the enjoyment of delusion." (57:20)

• Beautified for people is the love of that which they desire (3:14)

Allah has clarified that this life is only a stepping stone to the Hereafter, which is the true, ultimate, and everlasting life. The Prophet ﷺ informed his companion, Umar b. al-Khattab, of this when Umar entered upon him, and found him lying on a mat made from straw which had left marks on the Prophet's side. He said, "O Prophet of Allah, if you wish we can bring you bedding more comfortable than this." He replied:

"What do I need from this world? My example in this world is surely that of a person riding on a sunny day and then taking shade under a tree for a period of time, then leaving and continuing on his journey." (Ahmed)

Allah, the Almighty, has clarified to us that this life is full of worries and misery. If you feel joyful during one day, you will feel sorrowful on other days. If you laugh one day, you will cry on another day. Being joyous continually is not possible. This is the nature of this life.

It is inappropriate for any of us to rely upon this world and disregard the next. The Prophet ﷺ instructed his companion Abdullah b. Umar:

"Be in this life like a stranger or a traveler." (Bukhari)

The Muslim knows the shortness of this life, and this will increase his desire to attain more provisions for the Hereafter and to not blindly become attached to this life.

The kings, who one would think would certainly enjoy this life, don't enjoy it as some may perceive. Abdurrahman an-Nasir, one of the Umayyad Dynasty Caliphs of Spain, who ruled for over 50 years, wrote a note which was found near him when he died, "Indeed, the day that was truly a joyous day for this Caliph was such and such day from such and such month of such and such year." Altogether, there were fourteen days that he felt complete joy.

A poet clarified the nature of this life saying:

This life does not last for anyone
As you see, all things pass as quickly as they come,
Whoever is joyous for a period of time would feel sorrowful during many others

Another said:

Everyone you find complains about this life,
Woe to them, do they expect to live forever?

When the Muslim knows this, it will increase his desire to attain more provisions for the Hereafter and to not blindly become attached to this life. If this blind attachment to the world materializes, one will feel sorrowful for every missed opportunity and ultimately will ruin his happiness. Allah says:

"Every soul will taste death, and you will only be given your [full] compensation on the Day of Resurrection. So he who is drawn away from the Fire and admitted to Paradise has attained success. And what is the life of this world except the enjoyment of delusion." (3:185)

A good

companion will surely be a great help during times of hardship. He will help you when a disaster strikes and will remind you to be mindful of God when you forget.

06 One should accompany good individuals and avoid the company of those who are evil. No one can deny the influence a friend has over another. It has been said in the common parable, "The companion will drag you with him." Your friend will either drag you to goodness or to evil. He may be instrumental in you being happy or miserable. The Messenger of Allah ﷺ said:

"The example of a good companion and an evil one is like that of a perfume salesman and a blacksmith. A perfume salesman will either give you some perfume, sell it to you or at the very least you will smell a pleasant scent. On the other hand, a blacksmith will burn your clothes and in the very least you will smell a very unpleasant odor from him." (Bukhari)

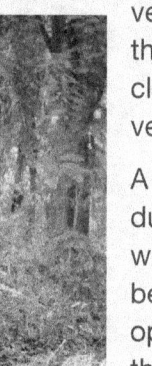

A good companion will surely be a great help during times of hardship. They will help you when a disaster strikes and will remind you to be mindful of God when you forget. This is the opposite of a bad companion, for he will be the first to abandon you when you are in need and will work to increase your misery.

07 Islam commands us to forsake sinful acts. Doing sinful acts will only bring misery to the individual and it will prevent him from experiencing true happiness. Ultimately, sinning will distance one from worshipping Allah, which is the very source of happiness. Allah says:

"No! Rather, a stain has covered their hearts as a result of that which they were earning." (83:14)

The Prophet ﷺ said:
"When a believer sins, it will be registered as a black dot on their heart. If he repents the black dot will be removed and his heart will be purified, but if he continues, the darkness will spread, and this is the stain that Allah speaks of in the Qur'an." (Ibn Majah)

A Muslim should refrain from sinning, for the Prophet ﷺ has clarified the dangers of sinning. He said:
"A man will be prevented from acquiring provisions on account of a sin that he does." (Ibn Hibban)

This feeling of misery is the result of one not being comfortable with the crime that they have committed. The Prophet ﷺ was once asked about sin and he replied, "Consult your soul, consult your heart. Righteousness is what is satisfying to your soul and your heart. Sin is what wavers in your soul and causes hesitancy in your chest, even if the people give you a verdict (that it's acceptable to do it), and again give you a verdict." (Sunan Ad-Darimi)

One should understand that this life is not a permanent place of stay. No matter how advanced we become, this world will come to an end.

08 One should be mindful of the previous nations and heed the punishments that befell them. One should understand that this life is not a permanent place of stay. No matter how advanced we become, this world will come to an end. Allah says:
"Have they not seen how many generations We destroyed before them which We had established upon the earth as We have not established you? And We sent [rain from] the sky upon them in showers and made rivers flow beneath them. Then We destroyed them for their sins and brought forth after them a generation of others." (6:6)

Allah says:
"Have they not traveled through the earth and observed what was the end of those before them? They were greater than them in power, and they plowed the earth and built it up more than they have built it up, and their messengers came to them with clear evidences. And Allah would not ever have wronged them, but they were wronging themselves." (30:9)

If one is in need, they should look at those who are less fortunate. If one is sick, but can move about, they should look at those who are bedridden.

Allah says:

"And [We destroyed the towns of] 'Aad and Thamud, and it has become clear to you from their [ruined] dwellings. And Satan had made pleasing to them their deeds and averted them from the path, and they were endowed with perception." (29:38)

Allah says:

"And how many a city have We destroyed that was insolent in its [way of] living, and those are their dwellings which have not been inhabited after them except briefly. And it is We who were the inheritors." (28:58)

When the Muslim realizes that this life is only a temporal stage, he would be happy and would submit to the will of Allah. Allah says: "And [O Muhammad] warn the people of a Day when the punishment will come to them and those who did wrong will say, 'Our Lord, delay us for a short term. We will answer Your call and follow the messengers.' [But it will be said], 'Had you not sworn, before, that for you there would be no cessation? And you lived among the dwellings of those who wronged themselves, and it had become clear to you how We dealt with them. And We presented for you [many] examples.'" (14:44-5)

09 **One should always look at those who are less fortunate.** Indeed, man is blessed with a wealth of blessings, but most often he is oblivious to them. One will only realize them when he loses them. If one is in need, they should look at those who are less fortunate. If one is sick, but can move about, they should look at those who are bedridden. The Prophet ﷺ said, "Look at those who are less fortunate than you. Do not look at those who are more fortunate than you, for this will cause one to despise the grace and blessing of Allah upon him." (Agreed Upon) If one is to look at those less fortunate than him, he will become satisfied and will recognize the grace of Allah upon him. A person came to a scholar complaining to him about the difficulty of his situation. The scholar asked him, "Would you want to exchange your eyesight for 100,000 silver coins?" The man replied, "Certainly not!" The scholar asked, "How about your hand for 100,000 silver coins?" He said, "Most certainly not!" The scholar asked, "How about your foot for 100,000 silver coins?" He responded, "Most certainly not!" The scholar then said, "I see in you graces and blessings worth hundreds of thousands of silver coins and yet you complain!"

In relation to issues that pertain to the Hereafter, one is always recommended to look at those who are better than himself, so that he can work on himself and improve.

The Qur'anic texts and the Prophetic Traditions have a great impact in fostering satisfaction in the hearts of Muslims. The reason for this is so that they can live a peaceful life, far from enmities and hatred.

10 Satisfaction is achieved when one is pleased with what Allah has ordained. When one distances himself from wanting what people have, and submits to the will of Allah, they will achieve pure satisfaction. The Qur'anic texts and the Prophetic Traditions have a great impact in fostering such satisfaction in the hearts of Muslims. This is so that they can live a peaceful life, far from envy and hatred, which would result when one is not satisfied. A person who is satisfied in the manner mentioned above will certainly live a happy life. Allah says: "And do not extend your eyes toward that by which We have given enjoyment to [some] categories of them, it is only but the splendor of worldly life by which We test them. And the provision of your Lord is better and more lasting." (20:131)

The Prophet ﷺ said:
"He who submits to Allah will be successful and his provisions will suffice him, and Allah will make him content with it." (Muslim)

The love of this world is a natural trait that everyone possesses, as the Messenger of Allah ﷺ informed us:
"If a person had two valleys of wealth, he would wish for a third equal to it. Nothing suffices the human being except soil[1], and Allah will forgive those who seek forgiveness." (Bukhari)

The Prophet ﷺ has instructed the Muslims to be content with

The Path To Happiness

The Prophet ﷺ said: "He who submits to Allah will be successful and his provisions will suffice him, and Allah will make him content with it."

what they have. This advice has a definite effect on the believers. He ﷺ said:

"Whoever among you wakes up secure in his home, healthy in his body, and having food for the day - it is as if he were given the entire world." (Tirmidthi)

If one is to carefully consider this Prophetic Tradition, he will realize that this is, in fact, all that he needs in life. As for the next day, the knowledge of it is with Allah, one does not have a guarantee that he will live to witness it or not. The money that is in one's account may not remain there as intended; a sudden event may come to pass and the savings could be lost. Allah says:

"Indeed, Allah [alone] has knowledge of the Hour and sends down the rain and knows what is in the wombs. And no soul perceives what it will earn tomorrow, and no soul perceives in what land it will die. Indeed, Allah is Knowing and Acquainted." (31:34)

11 **Submitting to the will of Allah and depending upon Him alone.** He is the One who takes care of all affairs. He gives to whomever He wills and withholds from whomever He wills. He makes powerful and noble whom He wills and makes weak and ignoble whom He wills. Allah says:

"Say, 'O Allah, Owner of Sovereignty, You give sovereignty to whom You will and You take sovereignty away from whom You will. You honor whom You will and You humble whom You will. In Your hand is all good. Indeed, You are over all things competent.'" (3:26)

You give sovereignty to whom You will. (3.26)

(1) This means a human will not be happy or content till he dies, at which point he will no longer harbor the desire to want worldly, material things.

When man knows that all the provisions have already been ordained and that this has been decreed from the time he was in the womb of his mother, he will not fret over lost opportunities. The Prophet ﷺ said:

"Verily the creation of each one of you is brought together in his mother's womb for forty days in the form a drop, then he becomes a clot of blood, then a chewed morsel of flesh. Then there is sent to him the Angel who breathes the soul into him and who is commanded with four matters: to write down his sustenance, his life span, his actions, and whether he will be happy or unhappy (whether or not he will enter Paradise)." (Bukhari)

No one will leave this life unless he receives all the possessions ordained for him by God. The Prophet ﷺ said:
"No individual will depart from this world until he completes the term (of life) assigned for him by Allah and until he takes all his provisions that are assigned to him; therefore, ask Allah. When the response to your supplication is delayed, do not seek what you want from unlawful sources, for one will only get the blessings of Allah when they obey Him." (Tabarani)

When man knows that all the provisions have already been ordained and that this has been decreed from the time he was in the womb of his mother, he will not fret over lost opportunities.

⑫ **One should be pleased with what Allah has assigned for him, even if these things may be seemingly bad for him.** Allah says:
"O you who have believed, it is not lawful for you to inherit women by compulsion. And do not make difficulties for them in order to take back part of what you gave them unless they commit a clear immorality. And live with them in kindness, for if you dislike them - perhaps you dislike a thing and Allah makes therein much good." (4:19)

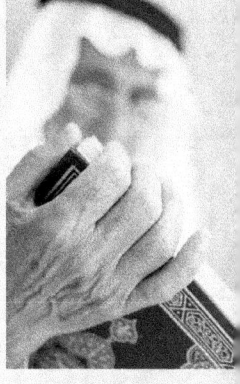

It may be that something you dislike may be good for you, and you would know not. Allah says:
"Fighting has been enjoined upon you while it is hateful to you. But perhaps you hate a thing and it is good for you, and perhaps you love a thing and it is bad for you. And Allah knows, while you know not." (2:216)

- And live with them in kindness (4:19)

One should know that Allah has favored some in terms of worldly, material possessions over others based on a divine wisdom.

 One should know that Allah has favored some in terms of worldly, material possessions over others based on a divine wisdom. Allah says:
"And Allah has favored some of you over others in provision. But those who were favored would not hand over their provision to their servants so they would be equal to them therein. Then is it the favor of Allah they reject?" (16:71)

Allah also says:
"Look how We have favored [in provision] some of you over others. But the Hereafter is greater in degrees [of difference] and greater in distinction." (17:21)

One should not envy others and desire what they have, nor should they aspire to lead a purely material life. Allah says:
"Say, 'Indeed, my Lord extends provision for whom He wills of His servants and restricts [it] for him. But whatever thing you spend [in His cause], He will compensate it; and He is the best of providers.'" (34:39)

Since wishful thinking of this nature is detrimental to satisfaction and contentment of the heart, Muslims have been instructed to avoid it. Allah says:
"And do not wish for that by which Allah has made some of you exceed others. For men is a share of what they have

• He is the best of providers (34:39)

earned and for women is a share of what they have earned and ask Allah of His bounty. Indeed, Allah is ever, of all things, Knowing." (4:32)

Instead of this, a Muslim has been ordered by Allah to closely examine what they have done and to keep themselves "in check". The Prophet said:
"The wise is he who keeps himself in check and scrutinizes what he has done and works for what comes after death. A failure is one who follows his whims and thinks wishfully of his abode while not working towards it." (Tirmidthi)

15. One should be careful to not become envious, hateful or hold grudges. These are dangerous sicknesses that will ruin one's feeling of happiness and replace it with misery. Whoever is not happy with what Allah has decreed for him and enviously desires what is in the hands of others will become hateful. Allah says:
"Or do they envy people for what Allah has given them of His bounty? But We had already given the family of Abraham the Scripture and wisdom, and conferred upon them a great kingdom." (4:54)

Arrogance resulting from envy was the first sin ever committed.

Arrogance resulting from envy was the first sin ever committed. Allah tells us what Iblis (Satan) did when God created Adam and ordered the Angels to bow down:
"[Iblis] said, 'Do You see this one whom You have honored above me? If You delay my death until the Day of Resurrection, I will surely destroy his descendants, except for a few.'" (17:62)

The Messenger of Allah spoke to his community, warning them of this disease:
"Do not envy one another, do not inflate prices for one another, do not hate one another, do not turn away from one another and do not undercut one another in trade. Rather, be servants of Allah and brothers. A Muslim is the brother of

a Muslim, he does not oppress him, nor does he fail him, nor does he lie to him, nor does he hold him in contempt. Piety is right here [and he pointed to his chest three times]. It is evil enough for a man to hold his fellow Muslim in contempt. A Muslim is sacred for another Muslim; his blood, his property, and his honor." (Muslim)

Allah instructs us to love for others what we love for ourselves. He says:

"And [there is a share for] those who came after them, saying, 'Our Lord, forgive us and our brothers who preceded us in faith and put not in our hearts [any] resentment toward those who have believed. Our Lord, indeed You Are Kind and Merciful.'" (59:10)

This feeling of good will and good fortune for one's fellow brothers should come from a sincere heart. The Prophet ﷺ said:

"Whoever supplicates for his brothers, an angel will say, 'Ameen and may you receive equal to it.'" (Muslim)

16 Avoiding arrogance and demeaning others. An arrogant person would not be happy, for people would despise him. He hates people and people hate him. How much happiness would such an individual experience? Allah says:

"Those who dispute concerning the signs of Allah without an authority having come to them, great is the hatred [of them] in the sight of Allah and in the sight of those who have believed. Thus does Allah seal over every heart [belonging to] an arrogant tyrant." (40:35)

• A Muslim is the brother of a Muslim

The Prophet ﷺ said:

"One who has an ant's weight of arrogance in his heart will not enter Paradise. A man said: 'O Messenger of Allah, one of us would like to wear good clothes and wear good sandals [is this arrogance?].' The Prophet ﷺ replied: 'Indeed Allah is beautiful and loves beauty. Arrogance is to reject the truth [out of pride] and to belittle people.'" (Muslim)

17 It is prohibited for one to be miserly. Miserliness is a trait that is despised in Islam and certainly is a chief cause in making one miserable. The miserly will always be worried about his wealth and will be fearful of losing any of it. The extra "care" he exercises will prevent him from enjoying his possessions and will also prevent him from giving out in the paths of goodness. Allah says:
"And let not those who [greedily] withhold what Allah has given them of His bounty ever think that it is better for them. Rather, it is worse for them. Their necks will be encircled by what they withheld on the Day of Resurrection. And to Allah belongs the heritage of the heavens and the earth. And Allah, with what you do, is [fully] Acquainted." (3:180)

Islam encourages the Muslim to give out in the path of Allah and not to be miserly. One who does not give out from his wealth, will ultimately lose his wealth.

The miserly will also distance himself from people, for he would fear that people would be after his money and worldly possessions. The Prophet ﷺ said:
"A generous person is beloved by Allah and beloved by people and would be protected from the Hell-Fire. The miser is not beloved by Allah and is far from Paradise, and disliked by people and close to the Hell-Fire. An ignorant, generous person is more beloved to Allah than a faithful miser." (Tirmidhi)

Islam encourages the Muslim to give in charity and not to be miserly. One who does not give out from his wealth will ultimately lose his wealth. The Prophet ﷺ said:
"Every day two angels will supplicate saying: 'O Allah give one who gives in charity for Your sake reward and bless his wealth, and make one who is a miser lose his wealth.'" (Bukhari)

The Path To Happiness

Patience is a requirement in our daily lives. In general, nothing can be acquired except with patience.

The Messenger of Allah clarified what dangers will afflict the community at large when miserliness becomes prevalent. The Prophet said:

"Beware of wrongdoing, for indeed it is a great darkness on the Day of Resurrection. Beware of miserliness, for it destroyed those who were before you. It led them to shedding each others blood and violating their families." (Muslim)

These traits are definitely despised in Islam and they are considered traits that decrease one's Iman (faith). The Prophet said:

"Belief in God and miserliness cannot coexist in an individual's heart." (Nasa'ee)

18 One is ordered to be patient and not lose hope regardless of what may befall them. Patience is a requirement in our daily lives. In general, nothing can be acquired except with patience. Allah says:

"O you who have believed, persevere and endure and remain stationed and fear Allah that you may be successful." (3:200)

This life is a test from Allah. He tests us to see who of us is most righteous. Allah says:

"And we will surely test you with something of fear and hunger, and a loss of wealth and lives and fruits, but give good tidings to the patient." (2:155)

• Obey Allah that you may be successful (3:200)

Along with patience, one is instructed to forgive one who has wronged him. Allah says:
"And whoever is patient and forgives - indeed, that is of the matters [requiring] determination." (42:43)

Becoming more patient is a goal every Muslim strives to attain. Allah has mentioned to us His love for those who are patient. Allah says:
"And Allah loves the patient." (3:146)

We are taught that when one holds patiently, they will find ease from the hardships that may have befallen them and they will find happiness after having been saddened by the calamity that befell them.

Allah has promised those who are patient with a complete reward. Allah says:
"Indeed, the patient will be given their reward without limit." (39:10)

The Prophet ﷺ said:
"There is no blessing greater than patience." (Bukhari & Muslim)

We are taught that when one holds patiently, they will find ease from the hardships that may have befallen them and they will find happiness after having been saddened by the calamity that befell them. Allah says:
"For indeed, with hardship [there will come] ease. Indeed, with hardship [there will come] ease." (94:5-6)

The Prophet ﷺ said:
"Know that victory is the outcome of patience, and that relief is the outcome of anguish and agony, and know that with hardship there is ease." (Hakim)

Patience is of three types:

First type: Patience when doing acts of worship. Allah says:
"Peace be upon you for what you patiently endured. And excellent is the final home." (13:24)

Second type: Patience in relation to avoiding sinful acts. Allah says:
"And keep yourself patient [by being] with those who call

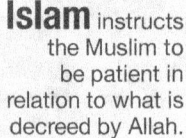

Islam instructs the Muslim to be patient in relation to what is decreed by Allah.

upon their Lord in the morning and the evening, seeking His countenance. And let not your eyes pass beyond them, desiring the adornments of the worldly life, and do not obey one whose heart We have made heedless of Our remembrance and who follows his desire and whose affair is ever [in] neglect." (18:28)

Third type: Patience in relation to calamities Allah decrees upon man. Allah says:
"No disaster strikes except by the permission of God. And whoever believes in Allah - He will guide his heart. And Allah is Knowing of all things." (64:11)

Islam instructs the Muslim to be patient in relation to what is decreed by Allah. We are instructed to say what the Prophet ﷺ has said when a calamity strikes:
"To Allah we belong and to Him we shall return. O Allah reward me in this calamity and give me better in return.' When one says this, Allah will reward him and give him better in return." (Ahmed)

19 One should not become angry or emotional. Anger will lead one to doing things that will make him sorrowful. Allah says:
"And those who avoid the major sins and immoralities, and when they are angry, they forgive." (42:37)

Whoever can control his anger will be able to undertake the hardships of this life; The Messenger of Allah ﷺ said:
"The powerful one is not one who can wrestle with another, but the powerful one is he who can control himself at the time of anger." (Agreed Upon)

20 We are encouraged in Islam to forgive when one wrongs us. This action will cause love to spread in the community. Allah says:

"Who spend [in the cause of Allah] during ease and hardship and who restrain anger and who pardon the people - and Allah loves the doers of good." (3:134)

We as Muslims have been ordered with something greater than all of this. We are to be kind when people are unkind towards us. This will rid an individual from the disease of hatred and fill him with happiness and the feeling of true brotherhood. Allah says:

"And not equal are the good deed and the bad. Repel evil by that [deed] which is better. And thereupon the one whom between you and him is enmity [will become] as though he was a devoted friend." (41:34)

21 The Muslim is ordered in Islam to be hopeful and not lose hope. The Prophet ﷺ was an example for all Muslims. He would love good omens and hate pessimism. (Bukhari)

22 One is forbidden to harbor evil thoughts or to spy on his fellow Muslims. Whoever thinks ill of people will live a worrisome life. He would be hated by people. Allah says:
"O you who have believed, avoid much [negative] assumption. Indeed, some assumption is sin. And do not spy or backbite each other. Would one of you like to eat the flesh of his brother when dead? You would detest it. And fear Allah, indeed, Allah is accepting of repentance and Merciful. O mankind, indeed We have created you from male and female and made you peoples and tribes that you may know one another. Indeed, the most noble of you in the sight of Allah is the most righteous of you. Indeed, Allah is Most Knowing and Acquainted." (49:12-13)

The Prophet ﷺ said:
"Beware of harboring evil thoughts, for it is the most untruthful form of speech. Do not spy on each other and do not be hateful. Be brothers in the sight of Allah." (Baihaqi)

We as Muslims have been ordered to be kind when people are unkind towards us. This will rid an individual from the filth of hatred and fill him with happiness and the feeling of true brotherhood.

We are also warned not to brag about what we have been given, for this will ruin the reward and will also rid us of happiness.

Harboring Good Thoughts

A Muslim is required to think well of what his fellow brother does and not interpret his actions to hold ill-meanings.

01 One should forget about the past and think of the present and leave the future to Allah. Allah says:
"Lest a soul should say, 'Oh [how great is] my regret over what I neglected in regard to Allah and that I was among the mockers.' Or [lest] one say, 'If only Allah had guided me, I would have been among the righteous.' Or [lest] one say when it sees the punishment, 'If only I had another turn so I could be among the doers of good.'" (39:56-58)

A famous writer wrote: "What has passed cannot be brought back. What you wish for is of the realm of the unseen. You have control over the things that happen in the hour that you are in. Thinking about the past will not bring it back, and thinking of the future will discourage you from doing what you have to do at present."

02 We are encouraged to give charitably and spend in the path of Allah. Indeed, happiness is in giving and not in receiving. After you do something beneficial, such as giving food to a poor person or giving clothing to a person in need of it, or helping someone out in a calamity, how do you feel? Allah says:
"And let not those of virtue and wealth among you swear not to give [aid] to their relatives and the needy and the emigrants for the cause of Allah, and let them pardon and overlook. Would you not like that Allah should forgive you? And Allah is Forgiving and Merciful." (24:22)

We are also warned to refrain from reminding those who received the charity of our generosity, whether these hints take

the form of words or actions, for this will ruin the reward and will also rid us of happiness. Allah says:
"O you who have believed, do not invalidate your charities with reminders [of it] or injury as does one who spends his wealth to be seen by the people and does not believe in Allah and the Last Day. His example is like that of a [large] smooth stone upon which is dust and is hit by a downpour that leaves it bare. They are unable [to keep] anything of what they have earned. And Allah does not guide the disbelieving people." (2:264)

The Muslim should be a positive factor in society, always keeping the commandments of Allah. Therefore, the Muslim should love goodness for others and hate evil for others.

If you do not have enough that you can give, then be kind in your speech and smile. It is indeed better than bragging for having given something out in the path of Allah. Allah says:
"Kind speech and forgiveness are better than charity followed by injury. And Allah is free of need and Forbearing." (2:263)

The Muslim should be a positive factor in society, always enforcing the commandments of Allah. Therefore, the Muslim should love goodness for others and hate evil for others. Allah says:
"And also for those who were settled in al-Madinah and [adopted] the faith before them. They love those who emigrated to them and find not any want in their hearts of what the emigrants were given but give [them] preference over themselves, even though they are in need. And whoever is protected from the stinginess of his soul - it is those who will be the successful." (59:9)

The Prophet ﷺ said:
"None of you truly believes until he loves for his brother what he loves for himself." (Bukhari)

03 **One should guide people to goodness and warn them from evil, so that they can live happy lives.** Allah says:
"And let there be arise from you a nation inviting to [all that is]

The Prophet said: "The most beloved people to Allah are the most beneficial to others. The most beloved deed to Allah is to make another Muslim happy."

good, enjoining what is right and forbidding what is wrong, and those will be the successful." (3:104)

The Prophet  said:

"The religion is based on sincerity and giving advice." We asked, "To whom?" He said, "Sincerity to Allah, His Book, and His Messenger, and sincere advice to the leaders of the Muslims and their common folk." (Muslim)

04 Helping the needy and giving out in charitable causes. Allah says:

"And those who are patient, seeking the countenance of their Lord, and establish prayer and spend from what We have provided for them secretly and publicly and prevent evil with good - those will have the good consequence of [this] home." (13:22)

05 One should intercede on behalf of others and use their influence to help others fulfill and complete things in goodness. Allah, the Exalted, says:

"Whoever intercedes for a good cause will have a reward therefrom, and whoever intercedes for an evil cause will have a burden therefrom. And ever is Allah, over all things, a Keeper." (4:85)

Whenever a person came to the Prophet asking him for something, he would say:

"Intercede for your brothers and you will receive reward. Allah will take care of your affairs." (Bukhari)

06 One should offer goodness to all people and in all forms. The Prophet said:

"The most beloved people to Allah are the most beneficial to others. The most beloved deed to Allah is to make another Muslim happy or to relieve him from a calamity or help him pay off a debt or to feed him when he is hungry. Helping someone is more beloved to me than secluding myself in worship in my mosque for a month. Whoever controls himself while they are angry, Allah will protect him. Whoever controls his anger, when he can inflict pain and harm upon someone else, Allah will fill his heart with happiness on the Day of Resurrection. Indeed, evil manners will destroy good deeds just as vinegar will spoil honey." (Tabarani)

When one strives to spread Islam, they will be in a state of happiness that cannot be described. When one saves another from the torment of Hell, it is indeed an amazing feeling. When one of the Companions of the Prophet Muhammad was asked by Rustum, the Persian King, why he had come to his lands, he replied, "We came to free people from worshipping humans so that they can worship the creator of the humans. We came to relieve people from the restrictions and limitations of this worldly life so that they can understand that the Hereafter is the real life. We came to free them from the oppression of all faiths to the justice of Islam."

Giving out in the path of Allah is not only in relation to Muslims. The Prophet ﷺ, also gave to non-Muslims.

"Anas b. Malik said that the Messenger of Allah was never asked a thing but he gave it. A person who accepted Islam went back to his people and said to them, "O People! Accept Islam, for indeed Muhammad gives out like a man who does not fear poverty." (Ibn Khuzaimah)

The Fourth Pillar: Belief in the Messengers of Allah.

They are the ones whom we are to emulate. One will not know Allah or reach ultimate happiness except through them. Imam Ibn al-Qayyim, said in his book Zaad al-Ma'ad:

"In relation to a cure that will cure the hearts, it can only be attained from what the Messengers delivered. Hearts would become well only by knowing their Creator and by striving to do the good and avoiding the unlawful that angers Allah. The heart

> **When** one believes in the Last Day, they will not be discomforted when they are unable to attain something in this life, for indeed better things are waiting for them in Heaven.

cannot become healthy except with this. One will not know any of this except through the revelation brought by the Messengers. Whoever thinks that they can achieve a healthy status without following the guidance delivered by them is indeed a fool. They would be living an animalistic life, following their desires and whims. Whoever cannot differentiate between these two states has a lifeless heart."

The Fifth Pillar: Belief in the Last Day.

When one believes in the Last Day and that people will be resurrected and then rewarded or punished, he will feel rested and assured that if he is oppressed in this life and cannot regain his rights, that Allah will give it to him in the Hereafter. In the Hereafter, payment is not with cash; rather, it is with deeds. The Prophet said to his Companions:

"Do you know who the 'bankrupt' is?" They said, "He is the one who has no money" The Prophet replied, "The bankrupt is he who comes from my nation with great deeds: prayers, fasting and charity, but having wronged so many that he would give those whom he wronged each of his good deeds, until all of them are finished. He would then take from their sins, and then be tossed into Hell." (Muslim)

Accountability and justice is not between mankind only, but also amongst the animals. The Prophet said:
"Rights will be given to their rightful owners. Even the right of a sheep that was gored by a ram will be taken as well." (Ibn Hibban)

When one believes in the Last Day, they will not be discomforted when they are unable to attain something in this life, for indeed better things are waiting for them in Heaven.

The Prophet said that Allah said:
"I have prepared for My believing slaves what no eye has seen, what no ear has heard about and what no mind has imagined." The Prophet then said, "Recite if you wish, 'And no soul

- The most beloved people to Allah are the most beneficial to others.

How to Attain True Happiness

knows what has been hidden for them of pleasure for their eyes as reward for what they used to do.'" (32:17)

When a calamity hits a believer, he bears it patiently, knowing it is a trial from Allah. All of the pain that he bore will be forgotten once he enters Paradise. The Prophet ﷺ said:
"The richest, most blessed person in this life will be brought forth and will be dipped into Hell and taken out, and then asked, 'O son of Adam, have you seen any goodness in your life?' He would say, 'No Allah!' Then the most miserable person in this life would be brought forth and he would be dipped into Heaven and then asked, 'Have you witnessed any hardship?' He would say, 'No Allah!'" (Muslim)

The belief in this pillar will cause the Muslim to strive in doing the good.

We believe that what has befallen us has been ordained by Allah, and what has missed us from a calamity or goodness would never be for us if Allah has not decreed it.

The Sixth Pillar: Belief in Preordainment.

We believe that what has befallen us has been ordained by Allah, and what has missed us from a calamity or goodness would never be for us if Allah has not decreed it. Allah says:
"No disaster strikes upon the earth or within yourselves except that it is in a register before We bring it into being – indeed that, for Allah, is easy. In order that you do not despair over what has eluded you, nor exult [in pride] over what He has given you. And Allah does not like the self-deluded and boastful." (57:22-23)

The Prophet ﷺ said to one of his companions:
"O young man, I shall teach you some words [of advice]: Be Mindful of Allah and Allah will protect you. If you ask, then ask Allah [alone], and if you seek help, then seek help from Allah [alone]. And know that if the Nation were to gather together to benefit you with anything, they would not benefit you except with what Allah had already ordained for you. And if they were to gather together to harm you with anything, they would not

- And Allah does not like the self-deluded and boastful. (57:22-23

The Path To Happiness

When one believes truthfully in this pillar (Belief in Preordainment) they will be able, by the will of Allah, to overcome their worries and concerns.

harm you except with what Allah had already ordained. The Pens have been lifted and the Pages have dried." (Hakim)

Belief in destiny will cause one to become happy and will put his heart at ease. One would not fret or become upset over lost chances. The Prophet ﷺ said:

"The strong believer is better and more beloved to Allah than the weak believer though in both there is goodness. Be careful to do that which is beneficial to you and do not despair. Indeed, that which has befallen you cannot be avoided so do not say, 'If I had done this or that,' for indeed 'if' opens the door to the devil." (Muslim)

One should not despair over a missed opportunity. If one is to actually take a moment and look at common ailments, it will be clear that the majority of diseases are on account of worries that are widespread. In other words, they are a result, whether direct or indirect, of disbelief in this pillar. When one believes truthfully in this pillar they will be able, by the will of Allah, to overcome their worries and concerns.

Types of Fear and its Cure:

Fears, concerns and worries have treatments and cures in Islam. A person may carry fear from certain things on account of a variety of things,

A Fear of not having enough provisions. Allah says:
"And in the heaven is your provision and whatever you are promised." (51:22)

Allah has told the truth. Indeed, in the heavens there is a provision for people. For example, rain falls and vegetation grows. People also benefit from the rainwater directly. Allah has promised to take care of the provisions for each individual. Allah says: "And there is no creature on earth but that upon Allah is its provision, and He knows its living and resting place. All is in a clear register." (11:6)

No matter how weak a creature is, his provisions are assigned to him by Allah. Allah says:
"And how many a creature carries not its [own] provision. Allah provides for it and for you. And He is the Hearing, the Knowing." (29:60)

We should strive to attain the provisions assigned to us by Allah. One should not be fearful that someone will prevent them from their assigned provisions.

Allah addressed Mary while she was in a state of weakness and pain during her labor with Jesus:

"And shake toward you the trunk of the palm tree. It will drop upon you ripe, fresh dates." (19:25)

Allah not only gave her dates, but fresh dates. All she had to do was shake the tree, and the dates fell within her reach.
Allah also has provided for the animals. They easily find means of sustenance wherever they are. The Prophet ﷺ said:
"If you were to truly depend upon Allah, He would provide for you as He provides for the birds. They leave their nests with empty stomachs and return with full stomachs." (Ibn Majah)

Many tend to depend upon God in the wrong way. In order for it be correct, one must do his part. The Prophet ﷺ once told a man who left his camel without tying it to a hitching post, wrongly thinking that this was "trusting in God":
"Tie your camel, and then trust Allah." (Ibn Hibban)

Many a time, some tend to neglect this and will simply want provisions to appear magically. The Prophet ﷺ said:
"If one of you were to sell firewood, it would be better for him than to beg." (Bukhari)

From this we understand that we should strive to attain the provisions assigned to us by Allah. One should not be fearful that someone will prevent them from their assigned provisions, for Allah says:
"Say [to them], 'If you possessed the depositories of the mercy of my Lord, then you would withhold out of fear of spending.' And ever has man been stingy." (17:100)

The Prophet ﷺ ordained that we accept the calamities that have befallen us and seek to alleviate them.

B. Fear of harmful things, such as sicknesses and calamities that may befall a person. No matter how a person worries over this, it will not change the matter in the least. On the contrary, it may even worsen his condition. Allah says:

"And if Allah should touch you with adversity, there is none to remove it except Him. And if He intends for you good, then there is none to block His bounty. He causes it to reach whom He wills of His servants. And He is the Forgiving, the Merciful." (10:107)

The Messenger of Allah ﷺ said:
"Amazing indeed is the attitude of the believer. All his affairs are ultimately good for him and this is only for a believer. When he is graced with a blessing, he would be grateful to God and it would be good for him, and when he is afflicted with a calamity, he would be patient and it would be good for him." (Muslim)

The Prophet ﷺ ordained that we accept the calamities that have befallen us and seek to alleviate them.

Once when the Prophet (ﷺ) went to visit his grandchild he shed some tears. He (ﷺ) sat with the child while he was on his deathbed. The child's eyes froze in their places like stones. Upon seeing that, the Prophet (ﷺ) wept. Sa'd said to him, in reference to the tears, "What is this 'O Prophet of God?" He replied, "This is a mercy that God, the Exalted, places in the hearts of His slaves. Truly, God is merciful to those who are merciful towards others." (Bukhari)

Patience is required of a Muslim and whoever falls sick is to seek medical attention. The Prophet ﷺ said:
"Seek medical attention O servants of Allah, for indeed Allah has not ordained a disease but there is a cure for it." (Ibn Hibban)

"Everyone upon the Earth will perish and there will remain your Lord, Owner of Majesty and Honor." (55:26)

One should be aware not to seek medical treatment from unlawful sources. Abu Hurairah said:
"The Messenger of Allah ﷺ forbade using medicines from unlawful sources." (Haakim)

He ﷺ also said:
"Every disease has a cure. Those who are ignorant of the cure would be ignorant of it, and those who know it will know it."
(Ibn Hibban)

> **What** a person should be concerned with is what is to come after death, not death itself. Trying to prevent death or finding cures for it is something that is futile.

C Fear of death. Death is a reality that everyone will experience. Allah says:
"Everyone upon the Earth will perish and there will remain the Face of your Lord, Owner of Majesty and Honor." (55:26)

No one can escape death. Allah says:
"Say, 'Indeed, the death from which you flee – indeed, it will meet you. Then you will be returned to the Knower of the unseen and the witnessed, and He will inform you about what you used to do.'" (62:8)

What a person should be concerned with is what is to come after death, not death itself. Trying to prevent death or finding cures for it is something that is futile. Allah says:
"And for every nation is a [specified] term. So when their time has come, they will not remain behind an hour, nor will they precede [it]." (7:34)

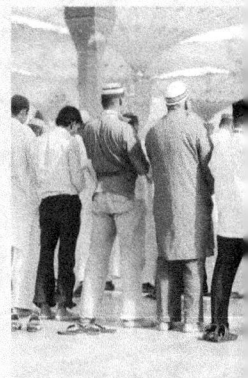

The one who hates death is one who has weak faith or no faith at all. When one believes in the Final Day, the Resurrection and the Account, they will certainly be at ease. A person who believes in death will work to better his situation after death and with this he will become a positive member of society. He will not be upset at chances that have passed or with the oppression of an oppressor, for all of them will be brought to account before Almighty Allah.

Final Thoughts

05

The Path To Happiness

Maurice Gaudefroy said: "Muhammad was a prophet, not a theologian, a fact so evident that one is loath to state it."

After this brief glance at Islam, if you were to ask me if I am convinced that Islam is the truth, I would say yes. The reason? I find it answers all the questions that come to my mind. I find it to be logical. I am at ease and feel comfortable with my belief, which includes the belief in Allah, doing that which I should do as a Muslim and refraining from the prohibited. With it, I am able to attain all my rights and find that the rights of others are preserved. In it, I find that Allah calls me to uphold good, ethical manners and to leave aside all unethical manners. If your belief doesn't give you all of this, then shouldn't you search for what is better?

Do you know what the best faith is? It is Islam. I am sure that some may say, "Well you are a Muslim and you are trying to market your faith!" But if I were to inform you that, not only Muslims profess this, but non-Muslims as well, what would you say? There are many Western writers who were fair in their approach and spoke nobly of Islam.

Maurice Gaudefroy said: "Muhammad was a prophet, not a theologian, a fact so evident that one is loath to state it. The men who surrounded him and constituted the influential elite of the [early] Muslim community, contented themselves with obeying the law that he had proclaimed in the name of Allah and with following his teaching and example."[1]

(1) Encyclopedia of Seerah by Afzalur-Rahman.

(2) He was a famous writer. He died in 1859.

(3) Encyclopedia of Seerah by Afzalur-Rahman.

(4) ibid.

Washington Irving[2], said: "His military triumphs awakened no pride nor vain glory as they would have done had they been effected by selfish purposes. In the time of his greatest power he maintained the same simplicity of manner and appearance as in the days of his adversity. So far from affecting regal state, he was displeased if, on entering a room, any unusual testimonial of respect was shown to him."[3]

Edmund Burke said: "The Muhammadan law, which is binding on all from the crowned head to the meanest subject, is a law interwoven with a system of the wisest, the most learned and the most enlightened jurisprudence that ever existed in the world."[4]

Final Thoughts

G. Margoliouth said: "The Koran admittedly occupies an important position among the great religious books of the world. Though the youngest of the epoch-making works belonging to this class of literature, it yields to hardly any in the wonderful effect which it has produced on large masses of men. It has created an all but new phase of human thought, and a fresh type of character."[1]

Now, to be frank, why don't you accept Islam as your faith?

 Is it because it calls to the Oneness of God?

 Is it because it calls upon people to worship Almighty God alone?

 Is it because it calls people to uphold all forms of ethics?

 Is it because it calls upon people to be just and avoid injustices?

 Is it because all people are considered equal in the sight of Allah?

 Is it because through it, all people will receive all their God-given rights?

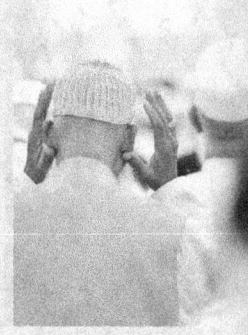

Since Islam came into existence some 1400 years ago till today, the number of people who are accepting it has increased. Whoever looks at it without preconceived notions and reads it with an open mind, will certainly be convinced and would accept Islam. If he does not accept it, they will at least appreciate it, respect it and not show hatred towards it.

Look at our situation today, with all the pressures and problems

(1) G. Margoliouth, Introduction to J. M. Rodwell's, The Koran (New York: Everyman's Library: 1977), vii.

The first step to accepting the truth is to listen objectively to what is being said. Ask God to help you and to guide you. When God sees in you the will to reach the truth, He will guide you.

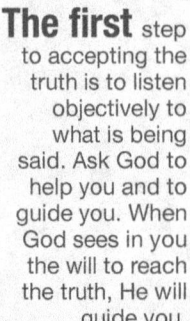

that have befallen the Muslims in all countries, they are still holding steadfast to their faith. In the former Soviet Union, Muslims were oppressed for seventy years. Their mosques were destroyed and their names changed. They were prevented from openly practicing their faith, yet, with the collapse of the Soviet Union, many Muslim-majority countries emerged. What does this prove? Doesn't it prove that Muslims are content, happy and firmly committed to their faith?

One who is fair and searches for the truth will certainly find nothing improper in the teachings of Islam. It calls people to uphold the highest manners, to become better and improve themselves. Some seekers of the truth have been through almost every faith, but have not considered Islam. I don't know what is preventing them? It may very well be that they will find happiness therein.

At times one is required to make a bold decision, a decision that will affect his future. The issue at hand is one of two: either that you accept Islam and achieve happiness, or that you don't accept it and stay as you are. Ask yourself, why is Islam being attacked seemingly every day in the media? It has been said, "man is enemy to that which he knows not," so don't hate something that you don't understand. Learn about Islam and share that knowledge so that no ignorant people will remain amongst us.

Steps to Accepting the Truth

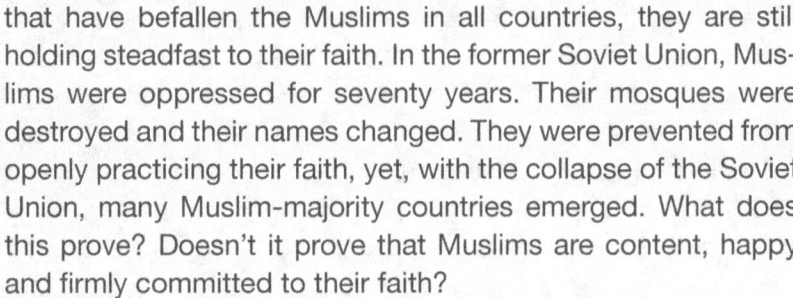

The first step to accepting the truth is to listen objectively to what is being said. Ask God to help you and to guide you. When God sees in you the sincere will to reach the truth, He will guide you. He says:
"And your Lord says, 'Call upon Me, I will respond to you.' Indeed, those who disdain My worship will enter Hell humiliated." (40:60)

Final Thoughts

Ask yourself why so many writers, thinkers and scholarly individuals from every country in the world have accepted Islam? The reason is quite simple. When they saw the integrity of Islam and its beauty after having read about it and having judged it for themselves without the influence of negative media. They made a decision on their own to accept Islam as their faith. They then experienced true happiness in their lives.

Some people though have read about Islam, understood it, but did not accept it. They spoke the truth in relation to the Qur'an and Islamic faith. Thomas Carlyle is an example. He said, "A false man found a religion? Why, a false man cannot build a brick house! If he does not know and follow truly the properties of mortar, burnt clay and what else he works in, it is no house that he makes, but a rubbish-heap. It will not stand for twelve centuries, to lodge a hundred and eighty million. It will fall straightway. A man must conform himself to Nature's laws, be verily in communion with Nature and the truth of things, or Nature will answer him, 'No, not at all!' Speciosities are specious – ah me! – a Cagliostro, many Cagliostro's, prominent world-leaders, do prosper by their quackery, for a day. It is like

George Bernard Shaw: "I have always held the religion of Muhammad in high estimation because of its wonderful vitality. It is the only religion which appears to possess that assimilating capability to the changing phases of existence which make itself appeal to every age."

The famous playwright and critic, George Bernard Shaw (d. 1950) said: "I have always held the religion of Muhammad in high estimation because of its wonderful vitality. It is the only religion which appears to possess that assimilating capability to the changing phases of existence which make itself appeal to every age – I have prophesized about the faith of Muhammad that it would be acceptable tomorrow as it is beginning to be acceptable to the Europe of today. Medieval ecclesiastics, either through ignorance or bigotry, painted [Islam] in the darkest colors. They were, in fact, trained to hate both the man Muhammad and his religion. To them, Muhammad was an anti-Christ. I have studied him, the wonderful man, and in my opinion, far from being an anti-Christ, he must be called the Saviour of humanity."[1]

(1) Heroes, Hero-Worship and the Heroic in History

Many Orientalists who studied Islam to attack it, actually ended up accepting it. Deborah Potter asserts: "This is because the evidence of the truth is decisive; there is no way to refute it."

a forged bank-note; they get it passed out of their worthless hands. Others, not they, have to smart for it.

Nature bursts up in fire-flames, French Revolutions and such like, proclaiming with terrible veracity that forged notes are forged. But of a Great Man especially, of him I will venture to assert that it is incredible he should have been other than true. It seems to me the primary foundation of him, and of all that can lie in him, this."[1]

Allah says:

"Indeed, [O Muhammad], you do not guide whom you like, but Allah guides whom He wills. And He is most knowing of the [rightly] guided." (28:56)

One cannot lose hope and say, "Maybe I am among those who will not be guided." No. As the Messenger of Allah ﷺ said: "Everyone from my community will enter Paradise except for those who refuse". He was asked: "Who will refuse?" He (ﷺ) said, "Whoever obeys me, shall enter Paradise, and whosoever disobeys me, refuses to (enter Paradise)." (Bukhari)

Many Orientalists who studied Islam to attack it, actually ended up accepting it. Deborah Potter[2] asserts: "Islam, which is the Law of God, is evident in nature around us. Mountains, oceans, planets and stars move in orbit by Allah's command. They are in a state of submission to the command of Allah, their Creator, as are characters in a story, and to Allah belongs the best example. They do not speak, nor act except with what the author decides for them. Like this, every atom in this universe, even of inanimate objects, is also in a state of submission.

(1) Encyclopedia of Seerah by Afzalur Rahman.

(2) Born in 1954 CE in Traverse, Michigan, she graduated from the University of Michigan in the field of Journalism. Taken from the book "What they say about Islam", by Imad-ud-Deen Khaleel.

However, humans are an exception to this rule, for Allah has granted him the freedom to choose. He has the option to submit to the command of Allah, or to lay down his own laws and invent the religion he pleases. Unfortunately, he has chosen the second option most of the time. People in Europe and America are embracing Islam in large numbers because they are thirsty for peace of mind and spiritual security. Rather, even a number of Christian

Orientalists and preachers, who originally commenced their work in order to destroy Islam and bring out its alleged shortcomings, have themselves become Muslims. This is because the evidence of the truth is decisive; there is no way to refute it."

All faiths today, except Islam, contain many reprehensible elements, practices and commands. They order their followers with things that are unacceptable. Each Prophet and Messenger was sent to their people in specific; whereas, Muhammad was sent to all of mankind.

> **Now,** looking at Muslims, you may see some who do not apply Islam as they should, but it doesn't mean that all Muslim are bad. In simple terms, judge Islam for what it is and not by what Muslims do.

A Doubt on Islam and Response:

Don't say, "If Islam were correct or as great as you say it is, Muslims would have adhered to their faith!" You may say this on account of a negative experience that you encountered with a Muslim, but have you gone through the same experience with every individual Muslim, so that you can stereotype the entire Muslim populace? Many Muslims apply Islam as they should, while others don't. Those who don't apply Islam as they should will receive due retribution from Allah.

Traffic lights have been set so that people drive in an orderly fashion. If a person goes through a red light, he will be putting himself and others at risk. Upon seeing one do this, is it fair that we issue a blanket ruling that all the people in that city are law breakers? Even if a person does get away with it a number of times, a person will ultimately get caught and be punished for what he has done. Now, looking at Muslims, you may see some who do not apply Islam as they should, but it doesn't mean that all Muslims are bad. In simple terms, judge Islam for its principles and not by what Muslims do. Islam is perfect but, Muslims are human and imperfect.

I know the decision of accepting Islam is a difficult one, and requires a degree of courage. I ask Allah, Almighty, to guide you to the truth and to open your heart to the truth and to guide you to attaining complete happiness. Amen.

www.ingramcontent.com/pod-product-compliance
Lightning Source LLC
LaVergne TN
LVHW020432080526
838202LV00055B/5156